Pure
Baking Soda

Over 100 Helpful Household Hints

Christine Halvorson

 Publications International, Ltd.

Writer
Christine Halvorson is the author of *Solve It With Salt & Vinegar,*
100s of Helpful Hints: Practical Uses for Arm & Hammer Baking Soda,
and *The Home Hints Calendar 2000,* and she is the coauthor of
Amazing Uses for Brand-Name Products and *Clean & Simple: A Back-*
to-Basics Approach to Cleaning Your Home. She is a frequent contribu-
tor to *The Old Farmer's Almanac* publications, including *Home*
Owner's Companion, Gardener's Companion, and *Good Cook's Com-*
panion. She works as a freelance writer from her home in Hancock,
New Hampshire.

Illustrations by Bot Roda.

Manufactured in China.

8 7 6 5 4 3 2 1

ISBN: 1-4127-1211-4

Contents

Introduction

In 1846, John Dwight and his brother-in-law, Dr. Austin Church, founded Church & Dwight Co., Inc., the manufacturer of ARM & HAMMER® Baking Soda. They began manufacturing and purifying sodium bicarbonate for use both commercially and in the house.

Baking soda is a naturally occurring, very versatile substance that's environmentally safe and inexpensive. Not only is baking soda nontoxic, it's actually a food so, unlike many commercial household products, it is safe to use around children and pets.

For this book, we've gathered more than 100 ways average people can—and do—use baking soda around the house. Whether in the kitchen, the bathroom, the laundry room, or even the garage, you'll be amazed at what baking soda can do.

BAKING SODA GUIDELINES

The hundreds of tips included in this book use baking soda in three different ways: directly; in a solution; and in a paste. Follow these guidelines for each of those uses when we don't otherwise supply specific measurements.

DIRECTLY

Baking soda is sprinkled directly onto something or onto a sponge. It is not diluted.

SOLUTION

Use 4 tablespoons baking soda for each quart of warm water. Sometimes solutions may contain a liquid other than water. Follow the directions carefully.

PASTE

To make a baking-soda paste, add just enough water to give it a consistency that will not run if applied to a vertical surface. Sometimes we may suggest pastes made of baking soda and a liquid other than water, such as lemon juice.

Clean and Fresh Kitchens

*B*aking soda can safely tackle kitchen jobs above and beyond the legendary box at the back of the refrigerator. Once you discover the  versatility of baking soda, you'll do away with all those cleaners under your sink, and you'll never use oven spray again. Of course, you can still use it for baking, but we'll leave those tips for "Cooking," beginning on page 51.

RUBBER, PLASTIC, AND WOOD

A baking-soda paste removes stains from plastic and rubber utensils. Apply with a scouring pad or sponge.

Scrub stained plastic storage containers with a paste of lemon juice and baking soda.

Renew old sponges, nylon scrubbers, and scrub brushes by soaking them overnight in a solution of 4 tablespoons baking soda to 1 quart water.

Deodorize and remove stains from wooden bowls or utensils with a baking-soda solution.

POTS, PANS, AND COOKWARE

Clean encrusted grease and food on roasting pans by dampening with hot water and sprinkling with baking soda. Let sit for an hour, and sponge clean.

To loosen baked- or dried-on food in pans, gently boil water and baking soda in the pans. When food is loosened, cool and wipe clean.

Enamel cookware can't handle abrasive cleaners. Apply a baking-soda paste and let sit for an hour, then clean with a synthetic scrubber, and rinse.

Remove stains from a nonstick pan by boiling 1 cup water, 2 tablespoons baking soda, and ½ cup liquid bleach in the pan for several minutes. Wash as usual, and use cooking oil to reseason.

Cover burned-on stains on cookie sheets with baking soda, then with hot water, and let soak for 10 minutes. Next, scour with baking soda and a scrubber.

SHINY SURFACES

Stainless-steel sinks and other surfaces can be cleaned with a baking-soda paste or by sprinkling baking soda directly onto a sponge or clean cloth and scrubbing the surface. Rinse and buff dry.

Clean the exterior of your refrigerator and most other surfaces in your kitchen using the General Purpose Cleanser. You'll find the recipe on the next page.

COUNTERTOPS

 Abrasive cleansers may scratch Formica. Instead, use the General Purpose Cleanser.

Remove stains on laminated countertops with a baking-soda paste. Apply, let dry, then rub off and rinse.

Clean a countertop made of tile and grout with a mixture of ½ cup vinegar, 1 cup clear ammonia, ¼ cup baking soda, and 1 gallon warm water. Apply with a sponge. Protect your hands with rubber gloves.

GENERAL PURPOSE CLEANSER

This homemade concoction can replace most of the commercial cleaners you probably have on your shelf.

1 tsp borax
1 tsp baking soda
2 tsp vinegar or lemon juice
¼ tsp liquid dish soap
2 cups hot water

Be sure to wear rubber gloves when working with this mixture. Mix and store in a squirt or spray bottle.

FLOORS

 Clean tile floors with ½ cup baking soda in a bucket of warm water. Mop and rinse clean.

Remove black heel marks on linoleum or vinyl floors with a damp sponge or scrubber dipped in baking soda.

OVENS AND STOVES

Clean induction and glass stovetops with a baking-soda solution, using a toothbrush to get into tight corners. Wipe clean.

For a thorough oven cleaning, leave 1 cup of ammonia in a cold, closed oven overnight to loosen dirt. In the morning, wipe away ammonia, then wipe surfaces with baking soda.

MORE TIPS AND TRICKS AROUND THE KITCHEN
COFFEE AND TEA

To clean teapots and stovetop percolators, fill with water, add 2 or 3 tablespoons of baking soda, and boil for 10 to 15 minutes. After cooling, scrub and rinse thoroughly.

Dip a damp sponge in baking soda and rub coffee cup and teacup stains away. Stubborn stains may also require a little salt.

To remove rust stains and mineral deposits from teapots, fill the pot with water, and add 2 tablespoons baking soda and the juice of half a lemon. Boil gently for 15 minutes, and rinse.

CLOG PREVENTION AND ELIMINATION

To prevent clogs, periodically pour ½ cup baking soda down your kitchen sink, followed by hot water. You can use the old box of baking soda from your refrigerator when you replace it.

Baking soda and vinegar will foam your drain clean and help prevent clogs. Use ½ cup baking soda, followed by 1 cup vinegar. When foam subsides, rinse with hot water.

GREASE CUTTER CLEANUP

Use this homemade solution to cut grease buildup on stoves, backsplashes, or glossy enamel surfaces.

¼ cup baking soda
½ cup white vinegar
1 cup ammonia
1 gallon hot water

Wear rubber gloves and use in a well-ventilated area.

OTHER HANDY TRICKS

Sprinkle baking soda on a damp sponge, and scrub your fruits and vegetables to remove dirt, wax, or pesticide residue. Rinse well.

Clean the oil out of a salad dressing cruet by shaking baking soda inside, then rinsing it clean with warm water.

GET THE SMELL OUT

REFRIGERATORS AND FREEZERS

An open box of baking soda in the refrigerator absorbs odors for up to three months. The same is true of freezers.

To remove any unpleasant taste in ice cubes from an automatic ice cube maker, clean removable parts of the unit with baking soda and water.

CUTTING BOARDS

Rub a wooden cutting board with a baking-soda paste to remove odors.

GARBAGE CANS

Reduce garbage-can smells by sprinkling baking soda in each time you add garbage.

Periodically wash out and deodorize garbage cans with a solution of 1 cup baking soda per 1 gallon water.

PUTTING OUT FIRES

Keep a box of baking soda within reach of the stove, but far enough away to be out of range of a fire. Pour baking soda directly on the flames to extinguish the fire.

Do not use baking soda to extinguish a fire in a deep fat fryer; the fat may splatter.

Do not use baking soda on any fire involving combustibles, such as wood or paper.

Do not hesitate to call 911 if you think the fire is out of hand.

When fire is extinguished, allow pots and their contents to cool before removing and cleaning.

You may want to keep an Emergency Fire Pail in your kitchen. Request a label with instructions on how to make one by sending a self-addressed, stamped envelope to ARM & HAMMER® Fire Pail Brochures, P.O. Box 7468, Princeton, NJ 08543.

Baking Soda Throughout the House

*E*ven the most meticulous housekeeper will find unwanted scuffs, smudges, and smells around every corner, in every room of the house. Whether it's cleaning windows or stained piano keys, removing water marks from a wood floor, or shining up the family silver and china, baking soda can be used in dozens of everyday household chores.

CLEANING WALLS AND OTHER SURFACES

 Remove crayon marks on walls with a damp sponge dipped in baking soda.

 Wax from dripped candles can be removed from most hard surfaces with a baking-soda paste. Scrub with a nylon scrubber.

A baking-soda paste is best for cleaning chrome surfaces. Apply, then buff dry.

Sprinkle baking soda directly onto stainless-steel surfaces, and clean with a damp sponge.

BASIC WALL CLEANER

Keep this mixture on hand for cleaning walls or other painted surfaces.

1 cup ammonia
1 cup baking soda
1 gallon water

Mix thoroughly, then apply with a sponge. Wear gloves to protect your hands from the ammonia. Scrub marks gently. Rinsing is unnecessary.

Scour soot and ash from fireplace bricks with a baking-soda solution. Rub into bricks with a stiff brush.

TABLETOPS AND WOOD

Remove alcohol stains from a wood table with a paste of baking soda and mineral, linseed, or lemon oil. Rub in the direction of the grain, then wipe with linseed oil.

Rub out white rings on wood tables with a paste made of equal amounts toothpaste and baking soda.

CARPETS AND FLOORS

Remove water spots on wood floors with a sponge dampened in a baking-soda solution.

Clean up pet accidents or vomit with baking soda. Scrub gently into rug with warm water, and brush. Vacuum when dry.

Control the odor from pet accidents by leaving a thin layer of baking soda after cleaning. Vacuum when dry.

Add baking soda to a vacuum bag to fight smells that can accumulate there.

UPHOLSTERY

A fresh stain of oily or greasy food on a cloth chair can be absorbed with equal parts baking soda and salt. Sprinkle, rub lightly, leave on for a few hours, then vacuum.

CARPET FRESHENER

1 cup crushed, dried herbs (rosemary, southernwood, lavender, etc.)
1 teaspoon ground cloves
1 teaspoon cinnamon
1 teaspoon baking soda

Combine ingredients, and sprinkle over carpet. Allow to sit for a few minutes, then vacuum.

CARPET FRESHENER VARIATIONS

Mix 1 small box baking soda with your favorite potpourri oil, using just a few drops, and sprinkle on as a carpet freshener. Leave on carpet 10 to 20 minutes, then vacuum.

Use 1 cup baking soda, 1 cup cornstarch, and 15 drops essential oil fragrance. Leave on carpet 10 to 20 minutes, then vacuum. Store mixture in a glass jar or airtight container.

Clean vinyl upholstery, such as a recliner or kitchen chair, with a baking-soda paste rubbed on, dried, then wiped off.

CONTROL HOUSEHOLD ODORS

Freshen blankets that have been in storage by sprinkling with baking soda and rolling them up for a couple of hours. Then fluff in the dryer without heat.

Before storing luggage or travel trunks, place an open box of baking soda inside, and close the luggage overnight. Repeat this when removing luggage from long-term storage.

If your waterbed mattress develops a musty odor, rinse it inside and out with a baking-soda solution, then refill as usual. Use a sponge to gently scrub the outside of the mattress with the solution.

Eliminate residue and smells from mops or rags by soaking them in a mixture of 4 tablespoons baking soda and 1 gallon water.

Fill the toes of old panty hose with baking soda, cut off the foot, and tie to secure. Hang the sachet to absorb musty odors.

JEWELRY

Clean gold and silver jewelry with 3 parts baking soda to 1 part water. Rub on gently, then rinse. Buff with a soft cloth.

Shine platinum jewelry with dry baking soda buffed on with a soft cloth.

GLASSWARE AND KNICKKNACKS

Clean stained china with a paste of baking soda and water.

To clean glass vases or other containers, fill three-quarters full with hot water, add a teaspoon of baking soda, and shake. Let sit, then rinse.

Stubborn spots on porcelain surfaces such as lamps, vases, and candlesticks can be cleaned by dipping a damp cloth in baking soda and rubbing.

WINDOWS AND BLINDS

Wash windows with a sponge dipped in baking soda. To avoid dry haze on the windows, rinse them with a clean sponge and plenty of water, and dry.

Put dirty venetian blinds in a tub of warm water and ½ cup baking soda, soak for half an hour, then scrub and rinse.

TIPS AND TRICKS

Once a month, sprinkle carpets with baking soda, let sit overnight, then vacuum.

Stained piano keys can be cleaned with a damp sponge dipped in baking soda. Wipe off, and buff.

Use baking soda to simulate snow on your Christmas tree.

A permanent filler for nail holes on white walls is a mixture of baking soda and white glue formed into paste.

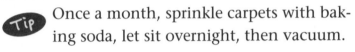

SILVER TARNISH REMOVER

Boil water and ½ teaspoon salt with 1 to 2 teaspoons of baking soda. Place tarnished silverware in pan with boiled mixture and a piece of aluminum foil. Simmer for 2 to 3 minutes. Rinse the silverware well, then use a soft cloth to buff dry.

Beautifying Your Bathroom

*F*or everyday cleaning in the bathroom, a sprinkling of baking soda on a damp sponge can often do the trick. Baking soda mixed with the right ingredients can clean mildew stains that plague tubs and showers and make your powder room smell clean and look shiny at all times without much effort.

TOILET

 A ½ cup of baking soda in the toilet bowl will work for light-duty cleaning. Let sit for 30 minutes, then brush.

Remove stubborn toilet stains by scrubbing with fine steel wool dipped in baking soda.

TUBS AND SHOWERS

Cleaning fiberglass tubs and showers requires a bit of caution since fiberglass scratches easily. Make a paste of baking soda and dishwashing liquid, and wipe on with a sponge.

BASIC BATHROOM CLEANER

3 tablespoons baking soda
½ cup ammonia
2 cups warm water

Mix and use for everyday cleaning. Be sure to wear rubber gloves, and use in a well-ventilated area.

VARIATION: THIS VERSION LEAVES OUT THE AMMONIA.

1 box (16 ounces) baking soda
4 tablespoons dishwashing liquid
1 cup warm water

Mix well, and store in a sealed container.

SOAP SCUM CLEANER

This mixture is great for removing soap scum buildup around your tub and sink.

¼ cup baking soda
½ cup vinegar
1 cup ammonia
1 gallon warm water

Mix well, and apply liberally. Wear rubber gloves. Make sure area is well ventilated. Rinse well.

Adding baking soda to bathwater will reduce ring-around-the-tub and soften your skin. Use 2 tablespoons for a tubful of water.

For tough grout or tile stains, use a paste of 1 part bleach to 3 parts baking soda.

Stains on nonskid strips or appliqués in the tub can be removed by dampening the area, then sprinkling with baking soda. Let sit for 20 minutes, then scrub and rinse.

Use a baking-soda paste to remove mildew stains on grout. Apply, scrub with an old toothbrush, and rinse.

Clean mildew stains and do light cleaning of a shower curtain by sprinkling baking soda on a sponge and scrubbing. Rinse well.

FLOORS

A tile or no-wax bathroom floor can be cleaned with ½ cup baking soda in a bucket of warm water. Mop and rinse.

DRAIN MAINTENANCE

For routine cleaning of sink and tub drains, pour in ½ cup baking soda followed by 1 cup vinegar. Let sit for 10 to 20 minutes, then flush with very hot water.

SHOWERHEAD TREATMENT

Remove mineral buildup and improve performance of your showerhead with this remedy.

½ cup baking soda
1 cup vinegar

Mix in a sturdy plastic bag, then secure the bag around the showerhead with a rubber band so that the showerhead is submerged in solution. Keep on, and soak for one hour. Remove, and run very hot water through the showerhead for several minutes.

ODOR CONTROL

Musty-smelling bath towels should be deodorized by machine washing. Add ½ cup baking soda to the rinse cycle.

Add a perpetual air freshener to the toilet area by keeping baking soda in a pretty dish on the back of the tank. Add your favorite scented bath salts to the mix, as well. Change every three months.

Add baking soda to the toe of old panty hose or nylon knee-highs, tie, and cut off the excess stocking. Hang around pipes under the sink for ongoing odor control.

Sprinkle baking soda in the bathroom trash can after each emptying.

COUNTERS AND VANITIES

Clean marble surfaces with a baking-soda-and-white-vinegar paste. Wipe clean, and buff.

A simple baking-soda paste will attack hard water or rust stains on ceramic tile. Use a nylon scrubber, then rinse.

Care for Clothing

*B*aking soda makes a great laundry product because of its mild alkali qualities. Dirt and grease are easily dissolved, while

clothes are softened. It is especially helpful in homes with hard water because it will not only clean clothes better, it will  prevent the stain buildup that can come with hard water, as well.

SMELLY HAMPERS

Freshen laundry hampers by sprinkling baking soda over dirty clothes as they await washing.

IN THE WASH

Add ½ cup baking soda with your detergent to freshen your laundry and help liquid detergents work harder.

Use baking soda instead of fabric softener. Add ½ cup at the rinse cycle.

BOOST YOUR BLEACH

Add ½ cup baking soda (only ¼ cup for front-loading machines) with the usual amount of bleach to increase whitening power.

PERSPIRATION STAINS

For perspiration stains, scrub in a paste of baking soda and water, let sit for 1 hour, then launder.

Treat stubborn perspiration stains around the collar with a paste of 4 tablespoons baking soda and ¼ cup water. Rub in, then add a little vinegar to the collar, and wash.

REMOVING ODORS

 Clothes can be deodorized by adding ½ cup baking soda to the rinse cycle.

Remove cigarette smoke smells in clothes by soaking them in a baking-soda solution before washing.

DELICATES

Eliminate the stale smell in stored-away handwashables by soaking in 4 tablespoons baking soda and a quart of water. Rinse well, squeeze, then air dry.

Prevent nylon items from yellowing by adding baking soda to both the wash and rinse water.

Yellowed linens can be brightened by adding 4 tablespoons baking soda to the wash water.

LAUNDRY ACCIDENTS

If you've washed a crayon in with a load of clothes, rewash the load with the hottest possible water, adding ½ to 1 full box of baking soda. Repeat if necessary.

If you've stained your white clothes by washing them with colored ones, undo the damage by soaking them in warm water to which you have added baking soda, salt, and detergent.

SPECIAL STAINS AND SPECIAL CLOTHING

Eliminate alcohol stains caused by perfume with a paste of baking soda and ammonia. Wear rubber gloves, and use this mixture in a well-ventilated area. Test for colorfastness first. Dry the fabric in the sun, then wash as usual.

PRETREATING STAIN REMOVER

½ cup ammonia
½ cup white vinegar
¼ cup baking soda
2 tablespoons liquid soap
2 quarts water

Mix all ingredients in a spray bottle. Spray the liquid onto the stain, and let it sit for a few minutes. Launder as usual.

A VARIATION: Use soap flakes and baking soda when washing stained natural fabrics. Add 1 tablespoon of vinegar to the rinse to keep colors bright.

To remove blood stains, dampen the area, then rub with baking soda. Follow by dabbing with hydrogen peroxide until the stain is gone. Test for colorfastness first.

Rinse pool chlorine out of bathing suits in a sink full of water with 1 tablespoon baking soda added.

Remove crayon marks on clothing by rubbing gently with baking soda sprinkled on a damp cloth.

The chemical finish in new clothes can bother sensitive skin. Soak them in water and ½ to 2 cups vinegar. Rinse. Then add ½ cup baking soda to the wash load.

DRY-CLEANABLES

Some dry-clean-only items can be cleaned with a solution of 4 tablespoons baking soda in cold water. Test for colorfastness first.

CLEANING WITHOUT WATER

Rub dry baking soda into polyester fabrics to remove a grease spot. Brush off, and the stain should be gone.

Clean suede with baking soda applied with a soft brush. Let it sit, and then brush it off.

LEATHER

An ink stain on leather can be removed by laying the item flat and sprinkling baking soda on the stain. Leave on until ink is absorbed, brush off, and repeat if necessary.

SHOES AND SOCKS

Remove black scuff marks on shoes with a baking-soda paste, rubbed on and wiped off, before applying polish.

Clean the rubber on athletic shoes with baking soda sprinkled on a sponge or washcloth.

Sprinkle baking soda into clean socks before wearing to control odor and moisture.

Keep smelly feet at bay by sprinkling baking soda into athletic shoes and street shoes to control odor and moisture.

Health and Beauty with Baking Soda

*O*nce upon a time, baking soda was one of the few products on the market for cleaning your teeth or settling an upset stomach. While we have many more choices today, baking soda still does the trick for these and dozens of other health and beauty tasks. Try it for shaving and shampooing, for minor burns and cuts, or for relaxation in the bath.

HAIR

SQUEAKY CLEAN HAIR

Add a teaspoon of baking soda to your usual shampoo bottle to help remove buildup from conditioners, mousses, and sprays, and to improve manageability.

In emergencies, use baking soda as a dry shampoo on oily hair. Sprinkle on and comb through, then fluff with a blow dryer.

CHLORINE REMOVER

Rinse hair with ½ teaspoon baking soda in 1 pint water to remove the dullness or discoloration caused by chlorinated pools.

COMBS AND BRUSHES

Hair spray and oil buildup on combs and brushes can be removed by soaking them in a sink of warm water and adding 3 tablespoons baking soda and 3 tablespoons bleach.

SKIN

HANDS AND ELBOWS

Remove fish, onion, or garlic odor from hands with a solution of 3 parts baking soda to 1 part water or liquid soap. Rub, and rinse.

Rub a baking-soda paste onto elbows to smooth away rough skin.

FEET

 Soak tired feet in a basin of warm water with 3 tablespoons baking soda.

Add 4 tablespoons baking soda to 1 quart warm water, and soak feet for 10 minutes to relieve foot itch.

Smooth rough and hardened calluses and heels by massaging with a paste of 3 parts baking soda per 1 part water.

RELAXING BATHS

Baking soda added to bathwater has a softening effect on the skin. Add ½ cup to a full bath, and soak.

Make bubbling bath salts with 2½ cups baking soda, 2 cups cream of tartar, and ½ cup cornstarch. Mix, and store in a covered container. Use ¼ cup per bath.

Relieve itchy wintery skin in a bath with 1 cup baking soda and 1¼ cups baby oil in the water.

NAIL CARE

 Clean fingernails and toenails by scrubbing with a nailbrush dipped in baking soda. This also softens cuticles.

SPONGE BATH

 Freshen up with a washcloth dipped in a solution of 4 tablespoons baking soda to 1 quart water.

DEODORANT

 Apply cornstarch to underarms with a powder puff first, then apply baking soda.

 For a simple daily deodorant, dust baking soda under arms using a powder puff.

TOOTH & MOUTH CARE

TOOTHPASTE

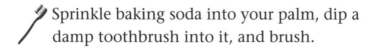 Mix 3 parts baking soda with 1 part salt. Add 3 teaspoons of glycerin. Add 10 to 20 drops of flavoring (peppermint, wintergreen, anise, or cinnamon) and enough water to make a paste. Spoon into a small, refillable squeeze bottle.

Sprinkle baking soda into your palm, dip a damp toothbrush into it, and brush.

REFRESHING MOUTHWASH

To freshen breath, use 1 teaspoon baking soda in ½ glass of water, swish the solution through your teeth, and rinse.

DENTURES AND OTHER DENTAL APPLIANCES

Soak dentures in a solution of 2 teaspoons baking soda dissolved in warm water.

Use baking soda to soak athletic mouth-guards, retainers, or other oral appliances.

Scrub dentures, mouthguards, and retainers with a toothbrush dipped in baking soda.

Soak toothbrushes in a baking-soda solution overnight.

FACE

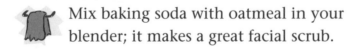

Make a paste of 3 parts baking soda to 1 part water, and use as a gentle, exfoliating facial scrub after washing with soap and water. Rinse clean.

Mix baking soda with oatmeal in your blender; it makes a great facial scrub.

SHAVING

 Men with sensitive skin may find that a solution of 1 tablespoon baking soda in 1 cup water makes a great preshave treatment or a soothing aftershave rinse.

For instant relief of razor burn, dab on a baking-soda solution.

SOOTHE MINOR MISHAPS

For sunburn pain, saturate a washcloth with a solution of 4 tablespoons baking soda in 1 quart water. Apply to affected area.

Ease windburn or poison ivy irritation with a paste of 3 parts baking soda and 1 part water. Do not use on broken skin.

ANTACID

Take ½ teaspoon baking soda in ½ glass of water to relieve acid indigestion or heartburn. Read antacid use information on the baking soda package before using. **WARNING:** *People who must restrict salt intake should not use baking soda as an antacid. Do not take for nausea, stomachache, gas, cramps, or distention from overeating.*

Dogs, Cats, and Other Critters

*B*aking soda is nontoxic and, therefore, safe for use around your dogs, cats, and other pets. It makes it easy to control odors and clean up accidents that are a natural part of having pets in the family. You can also use baking soda as a dry wash, to tend to bee stings, and to help maintain healthy teeth.

WASHING AND CLEANUP

BATHING

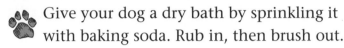 Give your dog a dry bath by sprinkling it with baking soda. Rub in, then brush out.

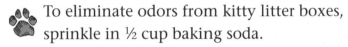 For a wet wash, combine 3 tablespoons baking soda with 1 teaspoon dishwashing liquid and 1 teaspoon baby oil in a spray bottle. Spritz your pet, then wipe dry.

KITTY LITTER

To eliminate odors from kitty litter boxes, sprinkle in ½ cup baking soda.

Make your own natural litter by mixing a small box of baking soda with 2 to 3 inches of dry, sandy clay.

Clean the kitty litter pan by removing litter and pouring in ½ inch vinegar. Let stand, then pour out, and dry. Sprinkle baking soda over the bottom before adding fresh kitty litter.

PET ACCIDENTS

To clean up after a pet's "accident," scrub the area with club soda, and let dry. Then sprinkle with baking soda, and let stand. Vacuum.

HEALTHY TEETH AND GUMS

You can brush your pet's teeth by dipping a damp, soft brush in baking soda and brushing gently.

Maintain your pet's dental hygiene by rinsing its mouth regularly with a solution of ½ teaspoon salt and ½ teaspoon baking soda in 1 cup warm water.

MORE TIPS AND TRICKS

SKUNKS

If your pet has a run-in with a skunk, wash the pet in a bath containing 1 quart 3-percent hydrogen peroxide, ¼ cup baking soda, and 1 teaspoon liquid soap. Rinse well, and dry. Discard unused cleaner.

BEE STING RELIEF

After making sure the stinger is removed, cover a bee sting on your pet with a baking-soda paste.

DEODORIZE BEDDING

Sprinkle the bedding area with baking soda, let stand, wait 15 minutes, and vacuum.

TOENAIL TRIMMING TIP

If you trim your pet's toenails yourself, you may accidentally draw blood by cutting too close to the quick. Dip the affected nail in baking soda, and apply pressure to stop bleeding.

OTHER CRITTERS

BIRDCAGE

Clean the bottom of your bird's cage by sprinkling baking soda on a damp sponge and scrubbing. Wipe clean to dry.

FERRET CAGE DEODORIZER

To reduce odors in a ferret cage, sprinkle a layer of baking soda over the bottom of the cage after cleaning. Cover with appropriate bedding.

SALTWATER AQUARIUM MAINTENANCE

To maintain the proper pH level in your saltwater aquarium, mix 1 tablespoon baking soda in 1 cup dechlorinated water. Add this to the tank slowly, over a couple hours, to attain the appropriate pH level for your fish.

Baby Care

Babies may be little, but the cleaning, deodorizing, and minor health challenges they present certainly aren't. Baking soda

can help you deal with this bundle of challenges. As an effective and inexpensive

product, it's safe for you and safe for baby. From deodorizing baby bottles to cleaning up the smell and mess of diapers and spit-up, baking soda can help.

CLEANING

Sprinkle baking soda on a damp sponge to wipe cribs, changing tables, baby mattresses, and playpens. Rinse thoroughly, and allow to dry.

Clean and deodorize baby spills or accidents on carpeting by soaking up as much as possible. When dry, sprinkle with baking soda, and let sit 15 minutes before vacuuming.

Use baking soda directly on metal, plastic, or vinyl strollers, car seats, and high chairs, using a damp sponge. Rinse, and wipe.

Remove odors from cloth strollers or car seats by sprinkling baking soda on the fabric. Wait 15 minutes, longer for strong odors, and vacuum.

When urine accidents occur on mattresses, sprinkle with baking soda, let dry thoroughly, then vacuum.

If your baby spits up on his shirt or yours, moisten a cloth, dip it in baking soda, and dab at the spot. The odor will be controlled until you can change.

Take a small spray bottle of a baking-soda solution with you on outings with baby for quick cleanups.

BABY COMBS

Rinse baby combs and brushes by swishing them in a small basin of water with 1 teaspoon baking soda. Rinse, and allow to dry.

TOY CARE

Clean and deodorize baby toys using a baking-soda solution. Wash toys with a damp sponge or cloth, rinse, and dry.

Cloth toys can get grungy. To clean without water, sprinkle on baking soda as a dry shampoo, let sit 15 minutes, then brush off.

Wipe vinyl toys clean with 1 tablespoon baking soda per cup of water. Remove stains with baking soda sprinkled on a damp sponge.

DEODORIZE

BABY BOTTLES

Fill bottles with warm water, and add 1 teaspoon baking soda. Shake, rinse, and then clean as usual.

Freshen bottle nipples and bottle brushes overnight by soaking in a mixture of 4 tablespoons baking soda per 1 quart hot water. Drain, rinse, and clean as normal in the morning.

DIAPER PAILS

 Keep diaper pails smelling fresh by sprinkling baking soda over dirty cloth diapers.

 Line the bottom of a diaper pail with baking soda to control odors after you empty it.

BABY LAUNDRY

Add ½ cup baking soda to powder or liquid laundry detergent to freshen clothes and help improve the detergent's performance on baby-food stains. With powder laundry detergent, add baking soda in the rinse cycle only.

Remove chemical finishes from new baby clothes by washing them first in mild soap and ½ cup baking soda.

TODDLERS

Use baking soda as toothpaste—or add a little to your child's regular toothpaste—to help take care of plaque buildup.

Baking Soda for Kids Big and Small

Mixing a liquid with a solid can form a gas. That may sound boring, but it can be a lot of fun to watch. The various chemical properties of baking soda make for some interesting rainy-day projects for kids and may just pique an interest in science. Build a volcano, make a picture frame, or create a piece of jewelry. Use these tips to demonstrate some basic principles or just to have fun.

JUMPING SEEDS

Dissolve ⅔ teaspoon baking soda in ½ cup water in a large glass. Add apple seeds from one apple and 1 tablespoon lemon juice, then stir the mixture. The bubbles will carry the seeds up and down.

MAGIC BEANS

Fill a vase with water, add food coloring and ¼ cup vinegar, then add 3 teaspoons baking soda. Drop in buttons, rice, or pasta, and watch them rise and fall like magic.

PLAY CLAY PROJECTS

FRAMEUPS

Capture a child's handprint in Play Clay (see recipe on the next page) by pressing into damp clay. When dry, paint and add the child's name and date on the back, then attach a picture hanger.

Cut a square or rectangle from Play Clay, then cut a frame opening the size of a favorite photograph. Leave a ½-inch border. Use another piece of clay for a stand to attach to the back. Decorate the frame.

PLAY CLAY

Make this clay, and then go wild with all the things you can create. The clay hardens as it dries for a lasting keepsake.

2 cups baking soda
1 cup cornstarch
1¼ cups cold water
    Food coloring (optional)

Mix baking soda and cornstarch in saucepan. Add water, stir to mix, then cook over medium heat, stirring constantly, 10 to 15 minutes. Add food coloring to the water to make colored clay. Don't overcook. Clay should have the consistency of mashed potatoes. Remove to a plate. Cover with a damp cloth to cool.

Make it ahead of time, and store it for up to one week. Keep it refrigerated in a plastic container, but bring it to room temperature before using.

THREE WAYS TO DRY PLAY CLAY ART
Air: Set on a wire rack overnight.

Oven: Preheat to 350°F, turn off, then place finished objects on a cooking sheet. Leave in until oven is cold.

Microwave: Place objects on a paper towel, bake at medium power for 30 seconds, turn over, bake for another 30 seconds. Repeat until dry.

Create a name plaque for a child's room by cutting out the shapes of letters and attaching them to a rectangular piece of Play Clay as the background. Paint and finish when dry.

JEWELRY

Shape beads for a necklace by rolling Play Clay into oval or round shapes. Press a toothpick through to make holes for stringing.

String Play Clay beads on thread, shoelaces, yarn, kite string, or fishing line. Tie knots between beads to hold them in place.

To make an earring or brooch, create small shapes with a flat backside, and glue to earring or pin backings.

PLAY CLAY HOLIDAY IDEAS

Make fancy napkin rings by rolling out a long, narrow rectangle of clay, then piecing the ends together into a ring.

Use cookie cutters to make tree ornaments. While the ornament is still wet, make a hole near the top for hanging. Add an ornament hook or ribbon to hang the ornament.

PLAY CLAY FINISHING TOUCHES

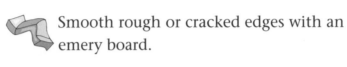 Paint dry pieces with watercolor, poster, or acrylic paints. Draw with felt-tip pen or waterproof marker. Apply glitter to wet paint.

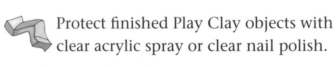 Smooth rough or cracked edges with an emery board.

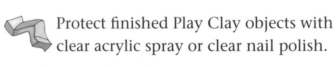 Protect finished Play Clay objects with clear acrylic spray or clear nail polish.

YOUR OWN VOLCANO

Shape a piece of cardboard into a cone. Insert a 4-ounce cup in the top of the cone to make the crater of the volcano. Stand the cone on a baking sheet. Cover the cone with plaster of paris. Don't get any in the cup. Let the cone dry completely. Paint or decorate the cone to look like a volcano.

MAKING THE ERUPTION

Mix ¼ cup vinegar with 1 teaspoon dishwashing liquid and a little red food coloring. Put 1 teaspoon baking soda into the crater cup. Pour the vinegar mixture into the crater.

VOLCANO VARIATION

Make a mini-volcano in a sandbox. Set a juice glass with vinegar in a mountain made of sand. Add 1 tablespoon baking soda to the glass.

Cooking

*I*f you've done nothing else with baking soda, you've probably baked with it. Baking soda is a great leavening agent when heated. It can be used to replace yeast in many recipes, and it can also help sweeten tart  fruits, fix some cooking mishaps, and perform tricks to make a good cook look like a better cook.

THE BASICS

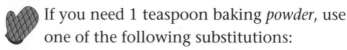 Test baking soda freshness by pouring a small amount of vinegar or lemon juice over ½ teaspoon of baking soda. If it doesn't actively bubble, it's too old to use.

A batter using baking soda should be mixed and put in the oven quickly to retain the best leavening action.

BAKING POWDER SUBSTITUTIONS

If you need 1 teaspoon baking *powder*, use one of the following substitutions:

¼ teaspoon baking soda plus ⅝ teaspoon (½ teaspoon plus ⅛ teaspoon) cream of tartar

¼ teaspoon baking soda plus ½ cup sour milk or buttermilk or yogurt (decrease liquid called for in recipe by ½ cup)

¼ teaspoon baking soda plus ½ tablespoon vinegar or lemon juice used with enough milk to make ½ cup (decrease liquid called for in recipe by ½ cup)

¼ teaspoon baking soda plus ¼ to ½ cup molasses (decrease liquid in recipe by 1 to 2 tablespoons)

OTHER SUBSTITUTIONS

Make self-rising flour with 3½ cups flour, 1¾ teaspoons baking powder, 1¾ teaspoons baking soda, and 1¾ teaspoons salt.

Yeast can be replaced in a recipe with equal parts baking soda and powdered vitamin C. The dough will rise during baking.

In a recipe calling for sour milk or buttermilk, substitute fresh milk, and add ¾ teaspoon baking soda to each cup needed.

To substitute honey for sugar in cookies, quick breads, or cakes, use ⅔ cup honey for each cup sugar. Add ½ teaspoon baking soda for every cup of honey. Reduce liquid by ¼ cup. Bake at 25 degrees less than the recipe recommends.

CAKES

Adding 1 teaspoon baking soda to the other dry ingredients in a chocolate cake will give the cake a darker color.

In a recipe for sour-cream cake, combining the baking soda and sour cream before mixing with other ingredients will activate the soda more quickly.

To prevent cracking in homemade frosting, add a pinch of baking soda before spreading it on a cake.

Substitute 1 teaspoon baking soda and 2 teaspoons vinegar for 2 eggs in any fruitcake or ginger cake recipe.

When making fruitcake, add a teaspoon of baking soda to darken the cake and soften the fruit a bit.

KITCHEN TRICKS

Add a pinch of baking soda to water when soaking dried beans. It helps make them more digestible.

Add 1 teaspoon baking soda to the cooking water for rice to improve fluffiness.

If you add too much vinegar to a recipe, add a pinch of baking soda to counteract.

Avoid lumps in batter by mixing baking soda with 1 teaspoon vinegar.

Omelets get fluffier if you add ½ teaspoon baking soda for every 3 eggs.

Add a pinch of baking soda to a buttermilk waffle recipe to make the waffles lighter and softer.

Avoid curdling boiled milk by adding a pinch of baking soda.

When gravy separates, a pinch of baking soda may get oils and fats to stick back together.

When making a boiled syrup, add a pinch of baking soda to prevent crystallizing.

MEAT, POULTRY, AND FISH

Tenderize tough meat by rubbing it with baking soda. Let it stand for several hours, then rinse and cook.

Rub baking soda into the fat surrounding pork chops to make them crispier.

Reduce fishy taste by soaking raw fish at least half an hour in 2 tablespoons baking soda and 1 quart water. Rinse, and cook.

Tenderize fowl by rubbing the cavity with baking soda, then refrigerating overnight.

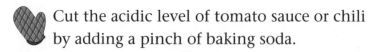 When scalding a whole, fresh chicken, add 1 teaspoon baking soda to the boiling water. Feathers will come off more easily, and the flesh will be clean and white.

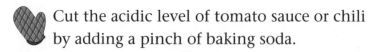 Before cooking poultry, rinse it in cold water and sprinkle baking soda inside and out. Rinse well.

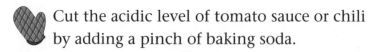 Soften the pungent taste of wild game by soaking it in baking soda and water overnight. Rinse and dry before cooking.

VEGETABLES

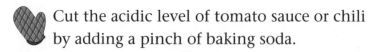 Add a pinch of baking soda to water when boiling cabbage to tenderize and avoid overcooking.

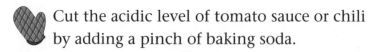 A pinch of baking soda thrown into potatoes while mashing will make them fluffier.

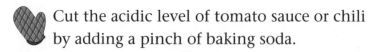 Test the acidic level of canned tomatoes. Dip a moist teaspoon in baking soda, then stir the tomatoes. Bubbling means their acid level is high.

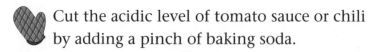 Cut the acidic level of tomato sauce or chili by adding a pinch of baking soda.

Eliminate the gaseous side effects of baked beans by adding a dash of baking soda while cooking.

Keep cauliflower white and its odor under control when boiling or steaming by adding 1 teaspoon baking soda.

FRUITS

Neutralize the acids in any recipe with a large amount of fruit by adding a pinch of baking soda.

When making fresh cranberry sauce, cover cranberries with water, and boil. Add 1 tablespoon baking soda, stir, drain, and return to heat. You'll need less sugar than usual to complete the sauce.

Tart blackberries can be sweetened by adding ½ teaspoon baking soda before adding any sugar when making pies or cobblers.

Soak rhubarb in cold water and a pinch of baking soda prior to making sauce. The water will turn black. Drain. You'll need less sugar in the sauce.

Sprinkle baking soda on fresh pineapple to improve its flavor, especially if the pineapple is not quite ripe.

LIQUIDS

Any time you might have to boil water before drinking it, soften it with 1 tablespoon baking soda per gallon of water.

Add a pinch of baking soda to a cup of coffee to reduce its acidity.

Add ¼ teaspoon baking soda to 8 ounces of orange juice, grapefruit juice, or lemonade, and stir. This will add a fizz to the drink and reduce its acidic level.

CANNING

Home-canned tomato juice may become too acidic. Add a bit of baking soda before using it in cooking to cut the acid level.

Clean mineral deposits and neutralize any acids in old canning jars by shaking a baking-soda solution inside. Rinse thoroughly, then sterilize as usual.

Outdoors and the Open Road

*B*aking soda's versatility makes it one of the best pieces of equipment to put in a backpack, boat, trunk, or garage. Closer to home it can clean your screens and aluminum siding and keep your garden green and thriving.

ON THE LAWN AND IN THE GARDEN
ACIDITY TEST FOR SOIL

To test the acidity level of your garden soil, add a pinch of baking soda to 1 tablespoon of soil. If it fizzes, the soil's pH level is probably less than 5.0.

Flower species that prefer alkaline soil such as geranium, begonia, and hydrangea should be watered occasionally with a weak baking-soda solution.

Sprinkle baking soda lightly around tomato plants. This will sweeten the tomatoes by lowering acidity.

RAISE ALKALINITY IN POTTED PLANT SOIL

Carnations, mums, and petunias prefer neutral soil. To raise potting soil alkalinity, apply a baking-soda solution. Use sparingly.

FLOWERS AND PLANTING POTS

Coat clay pots with a thin layer of baking soda when transplanting plants, before adding the soil. This helps keep dirt fresh.

Dip cut flowers in a solution of baking soda and water to lengthen their life.

ON THE DECK

Oily stains on deck wood from the grill or suntan lotion can be absorbed by sprinkling with baking soda and letting sit for 1 hour. Repeat if necessary.

PATIO FURNITURE

Clean lawn furniture at the start of the season with a solution of ¼ cup baking soda in 1 quart of warm water. Wipe, and rinse.

POOL TOYS

Remove mildew odors from plastic and vinyl pool toys with ¼ cup baking soda in 1 quart warm water.

GRILL CLEANING AND SAFETY

Loosen burned-on foods from barbecue grill racks by enclosing racks in a large plastic bag. Mix 1 cup baking soda and ½ cup ammonia, and pour over racks. Close the bag, and let it sit overnight.

Control the flames when fat drips on coals by keeping a spray bottle of 1 teaspoon baking soda mixed with 1 pint of water handy. Spray lightly onto coals when flames shoot up.

ON THE OPEN ROAD

RV OR BOAT HOLDING TANK

To dissolve solids and control odor in toilets of recreational vehicles or boats, pour a small box of baking soda into the tank after each cleaning.

RV WATER TANK

Deodorize and help remove mineral deposits in an RV water tank by flushing periodically with 1 cup baking soda in 1 gallon warm water. Drain, and flush the tank before refilling.

FISHING TRICKS

Keep fish hooks from rusting between fishing trips by sticking them in a cork and submerging the cork in baking soda.

Add baking soda to hollow fishing lures to give them spin in the water.

CLEANING OUT THE GARAGE

You can refresh musty old magazines found in cellars or garages if the pages aren't stuck together. Lay the magazines out in the sun for a day. Then sprinkle baking soda on the pages, and let sit for an hour or so. Brush off.

BATTERY TERMINALS

Neutralize acid from leaking batteries by applying baking soda to the spill. One pound of soda will neutralize 1 pint of acid.

GARAGE FLOORS

Mix equal parts baking soda and cornmeal to sprinkle on light oil spills in the garage. Let dry, then sweep or vacuum away.

For tougher spots on floors, sprinkle on baking soda, let stand, then scrub with a wet brush.

HOME MAINTENANCE

SCREENS

Dip a damp wire brush into baking soda, and scrub door and window screens clean, then rinse with a sponge or hose.

PAINTING

Soak brushes in a warm baking-soda solution to remove paint thinner.

Revive hardened paintbrush bristles by boiling them in ½ gallon water, 1 cup baking soda, and ¼ cup vinegar.

CARS

Use baking soda to safely clean lights, chrome, windows, tires, vinyl seats, and floormats in cars. Sprinkle onto a damp sponge, scrub, and rinse.

Other spots on upholstery can be cleaned with a baking-soda paste rubbed into the stain. Let dry, and vacuum.

Remove oil and grease on vinyl seats with a solution of baking soda and water, or with baking soda sprinkled on a damp sponge. Then rinse, and wipe.

REALLY ROUGHING IT

ALL-IN-ONE CAMPING TOOL

Take baking soda on camping trips to clean dishes, pots, hands, and teeth; to use as a deodorant and fire extinguisher; and to treat insect bites, sunburn, or poison ivy.

When camping season begins, deodorize sleeping bags by sprinkling in baking soda and letting them sit for half a day. Shake out, and set the sleeping bags in the sun.